Wanderlust:

(N.) A STRONG DESIRE FOR OR IMPULSE TO WANDER OR

TRAVEL AND EXPLORE THE WORLD

TRAVELLING MEMORIES OF

....

just in case

EMERGENCY CONTACT:

RELATION:

ADDRESS:

PHONE:

EMAIL:

BLOOD TYPE:

ALLERGIES:

VACCINATIONS:

DOCTOR'S NAME:

DOCTOR'S PHONE:

HEALTH INSURANCE:

POLICY #:

PHONE:

PASSPORT NUMBER:

ISSUED BY:

CREDIT CARD:

IF CARD IS LOST CALL:

LICENSE:

Adventure 1

destination research

LOCATION:

....

....

KNOWN FOR:

....

☐ ADVENTURE   ☐ BEACHES   ☐ FOOD & DRINK

☐ ARCHITECTURE   ☐ CULTURE   ☐ HISTORY

☐ ART & DESIGN   ☐ FAMILY FRIENDLY   ☐ SHOPPING

....

....

MUST DO ACTIVITIES:

....

....

....

....

....

....

....

....

....

....

....

....

....

....

....

....

....

....

packing list

- [ ] ....
- [ ] ....
- [ ] ....
- [ ] ....
- [ ] ....
- [ ] ....
- [ ] ....
- [ ] ....
- [ ] ....
- [ ] ....
- [ ] ....
- [ ] ....
- [ ] ....
- [ ] ....
- [ ] ....
- [ ] ....
- [ ] ....
- [ ] ....
- [ ] ....
- [ ] ....
- [ ] ....
- [ ] ....
- [ ] ....
- [ ] ....

to do before leaving

- [ ]
- [ ]
- [ ]
- [ ]
- [ ]
- [ ]
- [ ]
- [ ]
- [ ]
- [ ]
- [ ]
- [ ]
- [ ]
- [ ]
- [ ]
- [ ]
- [ ]
- [ ]
- [ ]
- [ ]
- [ ]
- [ ]

must see sights

accommodation wishlist

so & so told me...

I MUST SEE...

_____

_____

_____

_____

_____

_____

_____

_____

TO AVOID THE:

_____

_____

_____

_____

_____

_____

_____

_____

_____

_____

helpful websites

highlights

DATE: .... LOCATION: ....

WEATHER: ....

SLEEPING: ....

TODAY'S THREE GOOD THINGS: ....

....

....

....

WHERE I ATE: ....

....

....

....

ACTIVITIES: ....

....

....

....

UNFORGETABLE MOMENT: ....

....

....

....

....

highlights

DATE: .... LOCATION: ....

....

WEATHER: ....

SLEEPING: ....

....

TODAY'S THREE GOOD THINGS: ....

....

....

....

....

WHERE I ATE: ....

....

....

....

....

ACTIVITIES: ....

....

....

....

UNFORGETABLE MOMENT: ....

....

....

....

....

highlights

DATE: LOCATION:

WEATHER:

SLEEPING:

TODAY'S THREE GOOD THINGS:

WHERE I ATE:

ACTIVITIES:

UNFORGETABLE MOMENT:

highlights

DATE: .... LOCATION: ....

....

WEATHER: ....

SLEEPING: ....

....

TODAY'S THREE GOOD THINGS: ....

....

....

....

....

WHERE I ATE: ....

....

....

....

....

ACTIVITIES: ....

....

....

....

UNFORGETABLE MOMENT: ....

....

....

....

....

highlights

DATE: .... LOCATION: ....

WEATHER: ....

SLEEPING: ....

TODAY'S THREE GOOD THINGS: ....

....

....

....

WHERE I ATE: ....

....

....

....

ACTIVITIES: ....

....

....

....

UNFORGETABLE MOMENT: ....

....

....

....

....

magic moments

MOST MAGICAL DAY:

THE BEST MEAL:

HIGHLIGHT NATURAL WONDER:

MOST INCREDIBLE LOCATION:

MOST INTERESTING ENCOUNTER:

awakened spirit

WHAT OUTLOOKS OR PERSPECTIVES HAVE CHANGED ON THIS ADVENTURE?

journal

journal

journal

journal

journal

journal

journal

journal

notes

notes

notes

notes

Adventure 2

destination research

LOCATION:

KNOWN FOR:

☐ ADVENTURE ☐ BEACHES ☐ FOOD & DRINK

☐ ARCHITECTURE ☐ CULTURE ☐ HISTORY

☐ ART & DESIGN ☐ FAMILY FRIENDLY ☐ SHOPPING

MUST DO ACTIVITIES:

packing list

- [ ] ....
- [ ] ....
- [ ] ....
- [ ] ....
- [ ] ....
- [ ] ....
- [ ] ....
- [ ] ....
- [ ] ....
- [ ] ....
- [ ] ....
- [ ] ....
- [ ] ....
- [ ] ....
- [ ] ....
- [ ] ....
- [ ] ....
- [ ] ....
- [ ] ....
- [ ] ....
- [ ] ....
- [ ] ....
- [ ] ....
- [ ] ....

to do before leaving

- [ ]
- [ ]
- [ ]
- [ ]
- [ ]
- [ ]
- [ ]
- [ ]
- [ ]
- [ ]
- [ ]
- [ ]
- [ ]
- [ ]
- [ ]
- [ ]
- [ ]
- [ ]
- [ ]
- [ ]
- [ ]
- [ ]
- [ ]
- [ ]
- [ ]

must see sights

accommodation wishlist

so & so told me...

I MUST SEE...

....

....

....

....

....

....

....

....

....

TO AVOID THE:

....

....

....

....

....

....

....

....

....

....

....

helpful websites

highlights

DATE: .... LOCATION: ....

....

WEATHER: ....

SLEEPING: ....

....

TODAY'S THREE GOOD THINGS: ....

....

....

....

....

WHERE I ATE: ....

....

....

....

ACTIVITIES: ....

....

....

....

UNFORGETABLE MOMENT: ....

....

....

....

....

highlights

DATE: .... LOCATION: ....

WEATHER: ....

SLEEPING: ....

TODAY'S THREE GOOD THINGS: ....

....

....

....

WHERE I ATE: ....

....

....

....

ACTIVITIES: ....

....

....

UNFORGETABLE MOMENT: ....

....

....

....

....

highlights

DATE: LOCATION:

WEATHER:

SLEEPING:

TODAY'S THREE GOOD THINGS:

WHERE I ATE:

ACTIVITIES:

UNFORGETABLE MOMENT:

highlights

DATE: .... LOCATION: ....

....

WEATHER: ....

SLEEPING: ....

TODAY'S THREE GOOD THINGS: ....

....

....

....

WHERE I ATE: ....

....

....

....

ACTIVITIES: ....

....

....

UNFORGETABLE MOMENT: ....

....

....

....

....

highlights

DATE: .... LOCATION: ....

....

WEATHER: ....

SLEEPING: ....

....

TODAY'S THREE GOOD THINGS: ....

....

....

....

....

WHERE I ATE: ....

....

....

....

ACTIVITIES: ....

....

....

....

UNFORGETABLE MOMENT: ....

....

....

....

....

magic moments

MOST MAGICAL DAY:

THE BEST MEAL:

HIGHLIGHT NATURAL WONDER:

MOST INCREDIBLE LOCATION:

MOST INTERESTING ENCOUNTER:

awakened spirit

WHAT OUTLOOKS OR PERSPECTIVES HAVE CHANGED ON THIS ADVENTURE?

journal

journal

journal

journal

journal

journal

journal

journal

notes

notes

notes

notes

notes

Adventure 3

destination research

LOCATION:

KNOWN FOR:

☐ ADVENTURE   ☐ BEACHES   ☐ FOOD & DRINK

☐ ARCHITECTURE   ☐ CULTURE   ☐ HISTORY

☐ ART & DESIGN   ☐ FAMILY FRIENDLY   ☐ SHOPPING

MUST DO ACTIVITIES:

packing list

- [ ] ....
- [ ] ....
- [ ] ....
- [ ] ....
- [ ] ....
- [ ] ....
- [ ] ....
- [ ] ....
- [ ] ....
- [ ] ....
- [ ] ....
- [ ] ....
- [ ] ....
- [ ] ....
- [ ] ....
- [ ] ....
- [ ] ....
- [ ] ....
- [ ] ....
- [ ] ....
- [ ] ....
- [ ] ....

to do before leaving

- [ ]
- [ ]
- [ ]
- [ ]
- [ ]
- [ ]
- [ ]
- [ ]
- [ ]
- [ ]
- [ ]
- [ ]
- [ ]
- [ ]
- [ ]
- [ ]
- [ ]
- [ ]
- [ ]
- [ ]
- [ ]
- [ ]
- [ ]
- [ ]

must see sights

accommodation wishlist

so & so told me...

I MUST SEE...

TO AVOID THE:

helpful websites

highlights

DATE: .... LOCATION: ....

....

WEATHER: ....

SLEEPING: ....

....

TODAY'S THREE GOOD THINGS: ....

....

....

....

....

WHERE I ATE: ....

....

....

....

....

ACTIVITIES: ....

....

....

....

UNFORGETABLE MOMENT: ....

....

....

....

....

highlights

DATE: .... LOCATION: ....

....

WEATHER: ....

SLEEPING: ....

....

TODAY'S THREE GOOD THINGS: ....

....

....

....

....

WHERE I ATE: ....

....

....

....

....

ACTIVITIES: ....

....

....

....

UNFORGETABLE MOMENT: ....

....

....

....

....

highlights

DATE: .... LOCATION: ....

WEATHER: ....

SLEEPING: ....

TODAY'S THREE GOOD THINGS: ....

....

....

....

WHERE I ATE: ....

....

....

....

ACTIVITIES: ....

....

....

UNFORGETABLE MOMENT: ....

....

....

....

highlights

DATE: LOCATION:

WEATHER:

SLEEPING:

TODAY'S THREE GOOD THINGS:

WHERE I ATE:

ACTIVITIES:

UNFORGETABLE MOMENT:

highlights

DATE: .... LOCATION: ....

WEATHER: ....

SLEEPING: ....

TODAY'S THREE GOOD THINGS: ....

....

....

....

WHERE I ATE: ....

....

....

....

ACTIVITIES: ....

....

....

UNFORGETABLE MOMENT: ....

....

....

....

awakened spirit

WHAT OUTLOOKS OR PERSPECTIVES HAVE CHANGED ON THIS ADVENTURE?

journal

journal

journal

journal

journal

journal

journal

journal

notes

notes

notes

notes

notes

Dare to live the life you've always wanted.